GROUNDBREAKING WOMEN IN POLITICS

TAMMY DUCKWORTH

by Kelsey Jopp

FOCUS READERS®

VOYAGER

www.focusreaders.com

Focus Readers is distributed by North Star Editions:
sales@northstareditions.com | 888-417-0195

Produced for Focus Readers by Red Line Editorial.

Content Consultant: Christina Bejarano, Professor of Multicultural Women's and Gender Studies, Texas Woman's University

Photographs ©: Olivier Douliery/Abaca/Sipa USA/AP Images, cover, 1; Nam Y. Huh/AP Images, 4–5; Red Line Editorial, 7, 30; Fred Waters/AP Images, 8–9; Izabela23/Shutterstock Images, 11; Roman Babakin/Shutterstock Images, 13; Alan Budman/Shutterstock Images, 14–15; Sgt. 1st Class Andrew Kosterman/US Army/Defense Visual Information Distribution Service, 17; Staff Sgt. Robert Adams/Defense Visual Information Distribution Service, 19; David S. Holloway/Getty Images News/Getty Images, 20–21; John Gress/Reuters/Newscom, 23; Office of the Secretary of Defense Public Affairs/Defense Visual Information Distribution Services, 25; Kevin Lamarque/Reuters/Newscom, 27; George LeClaire/Daily Herald/AP Images, 28–29; Seth Perlman/AP Images, 33; Alex Brandon/AP Images, 34–35, 39; Pamela Brick/Shutterstock Images, 37; Jonathan Weiss/Shutterstock Images, 41; Brian Cassella/Chicago Tribune/TNS/Newscom, 42–43; Jonathan Ernst/Reuters/Newscom, 45

Library of Congress Cataloging-in-Publication Data
Names: Jopp, Kelsey, 1993- author.
Title: Tammy Duckworth / by Kelsey Jopp.
Description: Lake Elmo, MN : Focus Readers, 2020. | Series: Groundbreaking women in politics | Includes index. | Audience: Grades 4-6
Identifiers: LCCN 2019032500 (print) | LCCN 2019032501 (ebook) | ISBN 9781644930878 (hardcover) | ISBN 9781644931660 (paperback) | ISBN 9781644933244 (pdf) | ISBN 9781644932452 (ebook)
Subjects: LCSH: Duckworth, Tammy, 1968---Juvenile literature. | Women legislators--United States--Biography--Juvenile literature. | Legislators--United States--Biography--Juvenile literature. | United States. Congress. Senate--Biography--Juvenile literature.
Classification: LCC E840.8.D83 J67 2020 (print) | LCC E840.8.D83 (ebook) | DDC 328.73/092 [B]--dc23
LC record available at https://lccn.loc.gov/2019032500
LC ebook record available at https://lccn.loc.gov/2019032501

Printed in the United States of America
Mankato, MN
012020

ABOUT THE AUTHOR

Kelsey Jopp is an editor, writer, and lifelong learner. She lives in Saint Paul, Minnesota, where she enjoys practicing yoga and playing endless fetch with her sheltie, Teddy.

TABLE OF CONTENTS

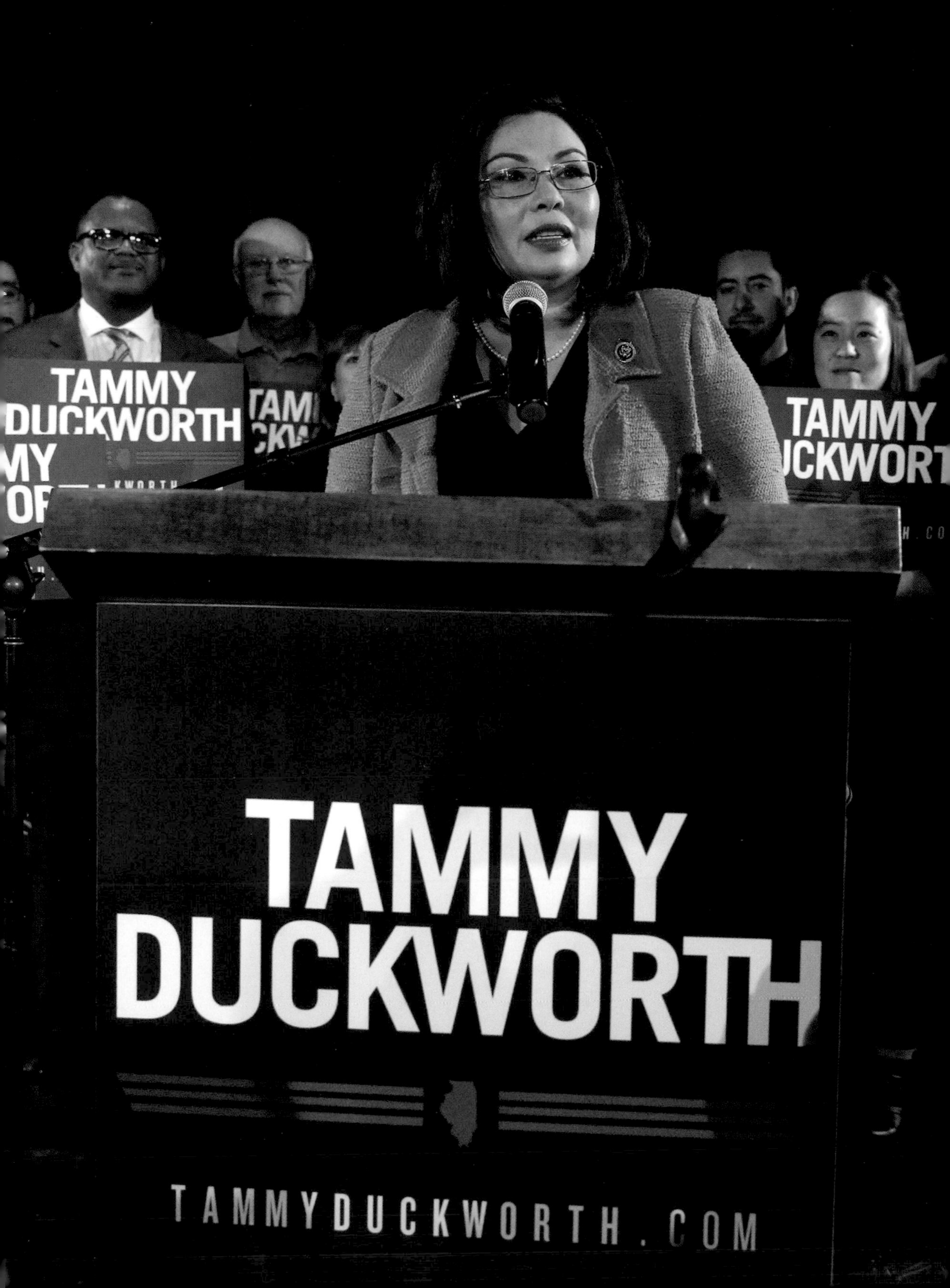

TAMMY
DUCKWORTH
TAMMYDUCKWORTH.COM

CHAPTER 1

A HEATED DEBATE

In October 2016, Tammy Duckworth neared the end of her election campaign. She was running to represent Illinois in the US Senate. Duckworth had been a member of the US House of Representatives since 2013.

Duckworth was running against **incumbent** Mark Kirk. He was a Republican. The Republican Party is one of two major US political parties. This party tends to support **conservative** policies.

Tammy Duckworth speaks after becoming the Democratic nominee for US Senate in March 2016.

Most Republicans believe in limited government, especially in terms of economic policies. Duckworth, on the other hand, was a Democrat. In general, this party supports **liberal** views. Democrats also tend to want greater government involvement, especially to support people in need.

On October 28, Duckworth and Kirk faced off in a debate. The election was less than two weeks away. In the debate, Duckworth discussed her family's long history of serving in the US military. In response, Kirk doubted her claims about her family. He made a joke about her ethnicity. Duckworth could have addressed the joke. However, she stayed focused on the debate. She talked about issues she cared about, such as foreign policy.

According to the **polls**, Duckworth was already in the lead. Kirk's comments during the debate did not help him make up any ground. Many people had found them disrespectful. On November 8, 2016, the people of Illinois voted for Duckworth to represent them. She became the second Asian American woman in history to serve as a US senator.

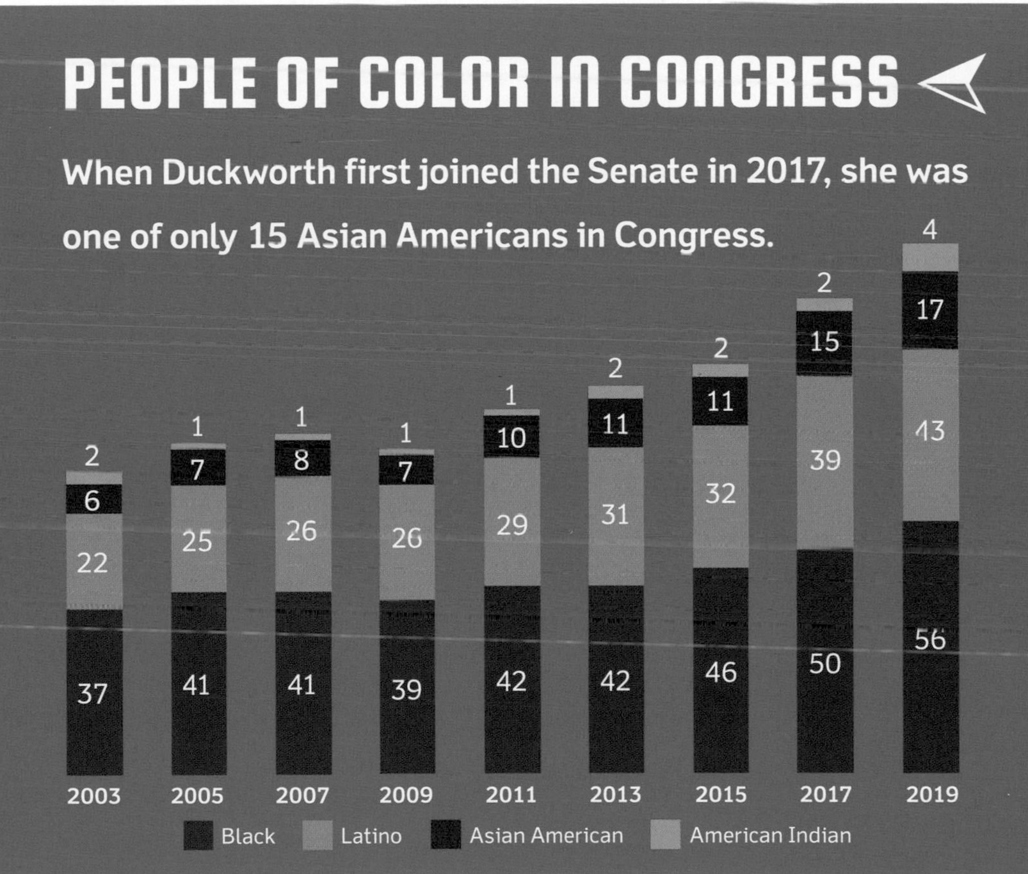

CHAPTER 2

LIFE ON THE MOVE

Tammy Duckworth was born in 1968 in Bangkok, Thailand. Her father, Franklin, was a US Marine. He had first moved to the region to serve in the Vietnam War (1954–1975). After serving, he got a job with the United Nations. This position led him to Thailand, where he helped **refugees**. During this time, he met Tammy's mother, Lamai, a Thai person with Chinese ancestry. She was working at her parents' store.

A refugee from Laos sits with her baby in Xieng Khong, Thailand, in 1962.

The couple got married and soon had Tammy. Later, her brother Thomas was born.

Tammy's family moved around a lot. Her father's work took them to countries all over Southeast Asia, including Thailand, Indonesia, Cambodia, and Singapore. Some of these countries were going through great political unrest. When Tammy lived in Cambodia, for example, the country was in the middle of a civil war. Tammy's mother would take Tammy to the roof of their home to watch bombs go off in the distance. She didn't want Tammy to be afraid of the loud noises, so she taught Tammy where they were coming from.

When Tammy was 16 years old, her father lost his job. Unsure what to do next, the family headed to the United States. However, since Tammy's mother was not a US citizen, she could not

Tammy Duckworth's family lived in Honolulu, the capital of Hawaii.

enter the country. Tammy and her brother were separated from their mother for six months. After working with the immigration system, Tammy's mother joined the family in Hawaii.

In Hawaii, the family's struggles grew worse. Tammy's father had trouble finding a job, and the family faced poverty. **Food stamps** helped the family survive. Tammy also took on several jobs to earn money for her family. One of her jobs was selling flowers on the side of the road.

Despite these challenges, Tammy excelled in school. She had skipped the ninth grade before moving to Hawaii, so she graduated from high school in just three years. She also excelled athletically, competing in volleyball and track.

Tammy's father eventually found work at a chicken factory. The summer before Tammy started college, her parents decided to save money by walking everywhere rather than riding the bus. They used their savings to pay Tammy's college expenses. Tammy also received grants and loans to fund her education. In 1989, she graduated from the University of Hawaii with a degree in political science.

THINK ABOUT IT

How did Tammy's childhood prepare her to become a politician?

Duckworth attended George Washington University for a master's degree in international affairs.

After graduation, Tammy Duckworth moved to Washington, DC, to study international affairs. She wanted to become a foreign **ambassador**. Her classmates encouraged her to join the military. They thought the experience would help her become an ambassador. Duckworth agreed. To understand foreign affairs, she needed to know how the military worked. Yet she didn't expect to love the military as much as she did.

CHAPTER 3

READY FOR BATTLE

Encouraged by her classmates, Tammy Duckworth joined the Reserve Officer Training Corps (ROTC) in 1990. ROTC prepares students to join the military. During this time, Duckworth also worked on Asian history exhibits at a nearby museum. She realized she wanted to study Asian history further.

To pursue these interests, Duckworth moved to Illinois to attend Northern Illinois University.

The US military usually offers scholarships to students who enroll in ROTC.

This school had a strong program on Southeast Asia. Duckworth also continued her ROTC training at the school. In Illinois, she discovered her love for the Midwest. She had been on the move for years. She felt like Illinois was home.

In 1992, Duckworth joined the Army Reserves. After joining, Duckworth had to choose an assignment in the military. Helicopter piloting was one of the only **combat** positions open to women. Duckworth wanted to see action in the army. She wanted to face the same risks that men faced. To become a pilot, Duckworth left her history program in Illinois. She went to flight school at Fort Rucker, Alabama.

At flight school, Duckworth was the only woman in her unit. She worked hard to prove herself. She graduated in the top three of her class. These top three pilots got to fly Black Hawk

A pilot flies a Black Hawk helicopter at Fort Rucker, Alabama.

helicopters. The military uses Black Hawks to carry supplies to the battlefield. Piloting them can be a very dangerous job.

For many years, Duckworth did not see much action. In 1995, her Army Reserves unit was deactivated. She switched to the National Guard. Soldiers in the National Guard report for national and state missions. In contrast, soldiers in the Army Reserves report on only the national level.

State missions in the National Guard do not involve combat. Duckworth's move meant she had even less chance of seeing action.

From 1996 to 2003, she moved up in the National Guard. She also continued her education in Illinois. Then, in 2004, Duckworth's dream to enter combat finally came true. She was **deployed** to Iraq.

After less than a year in Iraq, disaster struck. On November 12, 2004, Duckworth was copiloting a Black Hawk when a grenade exploded beneath the helicopter. Enemies were attacking. Duckworth tried to take control of the Black Hawk, but she could not feel her feet. The other pilot landed the helicopter. When they reached the ground, Duckworth passed out.

A response team rushed Duckworth to the hospital, where doctors amputated, or removed,

By 2000, Duckworth had become a captain in the Illinois Army National Guard.

both her legs. Duckworth knew she was lucky to be alive. However, recovery would not be an easy process. In addition, without her legs, she would no longer be able to serve in combat. An important era of her life was over, but Duckworth set her sights on the future.

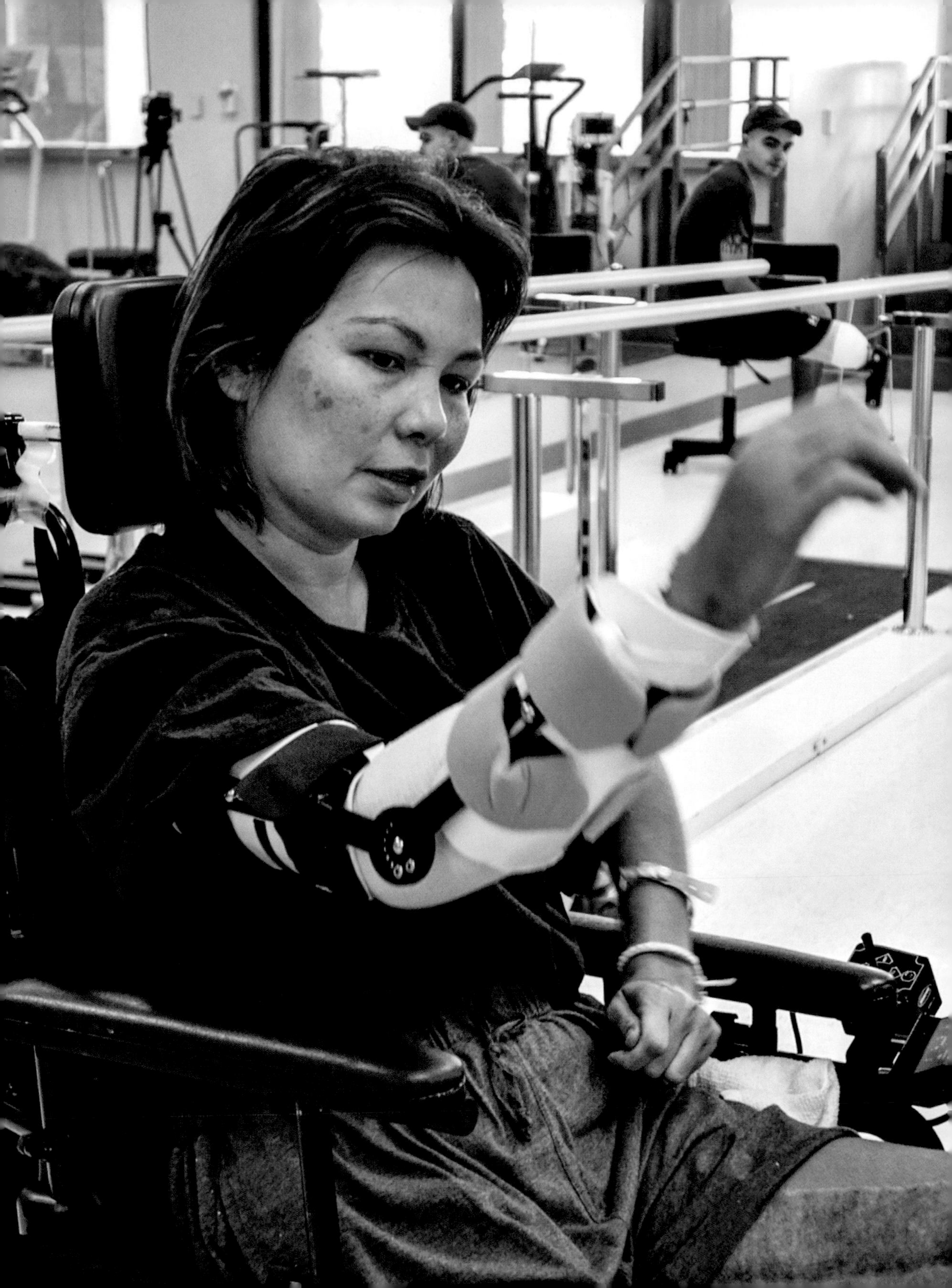

CHAPTER 4

BREAKING INTO POLITICS

Tammy Duckworth recovered from her injuries at Walter Reed National Military Medical Center in Maryland. She stayed at Walter Reed for a year. During this time, she learned to use her **prosthetic** legs. She also met several politicians. They often visited Walter Reed to meet with veterans. Many of the politicians cared about helping veterans. They also hoped to earn veterans' votes.

Tammy Duckworth recovers at Walter Reed National Military Medical Center.

Illinois Senator Dick Durbin was one of these visitors. Durbin noticed that Duckworth often offered support to other veterans. In her time at Walter Reed, Duckworth had become an activist for veterans' affairs. She thought wounded soldiers and their families deserved better medical care. Duckworth's passion impressed Durbin. He recommended she run for office. He even invited her to the 2005 State of the Union address. At this event, the US president talks about issues facing the country.

The event sparked Duckworth's interest in politics. She took Durbin's advice and ran for Congress in 2006. The US Congress makes the nation's laws. It is made up of two bodies, the Senate and the House of Representatives. Duckworth ran for the House of Representatives. She ran to represent Illinois's Sixth District.

Illinois Senators Barack Obama (left) and Dick Durbin campaigned for Duckworth during her 2006 House run.

Because Duckworth had attended school in Illinois, she felt a close connection to the state. Duckworth lost the race by fewer than 5,000 votes. The seat went to Republican Peter Roskam instead.

Duckworth was devastated by the loss, but she did not stay down for long. She found a new opportunity soon after losing the election.

From 2006 to 2009, Duckworth directed the Illinois Department of Veterans' Affairs. She started a program that encouraged businesses to hire veterans. If a business in this program hired a veteran, the business owed fewer taxes. Duckworth also started a mental health hotline for veterans. Veterans could call the hotline for help if they were struggling with their mental health. Another program helped nurses at veterans' centers pay off school debt. This program tried to get more nurses to work in veterans' affairs.

In 2009, President Barack Obama appointed Duckworth to the federal Department of Veterans'

THINK ABOUT IT

How do you think Duckworth benefited from losing the 2006 race? How did she become a stronger political candidate after that loss?

In 2009, Duckworth was sworn in as assistant secretary of the federal Department of Veterans' Affairs.

Affairs. In her new job, Duckworth worked on public relations projects. For example, she worked on raising awareness of government services for veterans.

By 2012, Duckworth had worked in veterans' affairs for six years. She had proved herself as both a soldier and a politician. With more experience behind her, Duckworth was ready to run for Congress again.

VETERANS' AFFAIRS

Tammy Duckworth built her career helping military members. She knew firsthand about the problems veterans face. After her recovery in 2004, she was determined to help.

One of the largest issues facing veterans is mental illness. Serving in combat is very stressful. Combat often causes trauma, or deep emotional pain. Veterans may struggle with depression or other mental illnesses. Because of these struggles, they are twice as likely as nonveterans to die by suicide.

Veterans also face a greater risk of experiencing homelessness. Many people struggle to find jobs after leaving the military. They are also more likely than nonveterans to have problems with alcohol and drug use. These problems can make it hard to earn money. As a result, veterans may not be able to pay for a home.

Tammy Duckworth meets with a veteran of World War II (1939–1945) and looks through his scrapbook.

In response to these issues, Duckworth started many programs to support veterans. In Illinois, she worked to improve health care for veterans. She also worked to connect veterans with housing resources. On the national level, she continued this work. In 2019, she put forward a **bill** to support female veterans. It would offer money to female veterans in poverty. The bill would also increase mental health services for these women.

CHAPTER 5

MOVING UP

In 2012, Tammy Duckworth ran again for the House of Representatives. This time, she ran in Illinois's Eighth District. Her opponent, Joe Walsh, already held the seat. However, he was losing favor with voters. At a campaign event, Walsh said Duckworth talked too much about her military service. He said true heroes did not talk about their service. Many voters found these comments disrespectful. They voted for Duckworth instead.

Tammy Duckworth meets with supporters after winning her 2012 congressional race.

Duckworth won the race with more than 54 percent of the votes. She had finally made it to Congress. In addition, more women had been elected to the House than ever before. Duckworth was part of a growing movement to better represent women in Congress.

WOMEN IN THE HOUSE

In 2012, Duckworth was one of a record 78 women elected to the US House of Representatives.

In her first four years on the job, Duckworth worked to pass several important laws. One of these laws was the Clay Hunt Act. This law aims to reduce suicide among veterans. Duckworth saw this bill become a law during her first term in the House. This achievement was a sign of success for first-term members.

In March 2015, Duckworth felt she was prepared to take another important step in her career. That month, she announced that she was running for US senator. Like the House, the Senate makes laws. However, the Senate is known as the upper house. It has only 100 members serving six-year terms. The House is known as the lower house. It has 435 members serving two-year terms. For these reasons, many people consider senators to be more important than members of the House.

Becoming a senator is no easy task. However, Duckworth had advantages over her opponent. She was running against Republican Mark Kirk. Many experts believed Kirk was the most likely senator to lose his position in the 2016 election. Illinois voters tended to elect Democrats. Since Duckworth was a Democrat, she had a better chance of winning.

At the same time, Duckworth faced criticism about her job performance. She had taken on many important projects. But her opponents questioned the success of these programs. For example, her veteran programs in Illinois failed to bring in many participants. Only 12 companies took part in Duckworth's tax-benefit program during its first year. And fewer than 20 nurses used the debt repayment program. Even fewer nurses used the program in its second year.

Duckworth faces off with Mark Kirk in a debate during her 2016 campaign for the US Senate.

Duckworth defended her work. She said that if a program helped just one veteran, it was a success. Duckworth also focused on her commitment to veterans. In the end, her strengths overcame her weaknesses. In November 2016, Illinois voters elected Duckworth to the US Senate.

CHAPTER 6

SUCCESS IN THE SENATE

After becoming a senator, Tammy Duckworth introduced many bills. She set a record among the other senators in office at the time. She was the fastest to pass a bill after taking office. Her first bill became law only four months after she was sworn in. Law S. 496 kept governors of other states from delaying work on Illinois roads and bridges. Experts thought it would save Illinois taxpayers more than $80 million per year.

On January 3, 2017, Tammy Duckworth was sworn in to the US Senate.

The law would also support Illinois citizens by creating more jobs.

Duckworth passed other successful bills. One was the Veterans Small Business Enhancement Act. This law allows veterans who own small businesses to use equipment or property that the government no longer needs. The law was designed to help veterans start businesses. Duckworth also passed the Friendly Airports for Mothers (FAM) Act. FAM requires airports to provide rooms where mothers can breastfeed their babies. The law also requires airports to provide diaper-changing tables in men's and women's bathrooms.

Duckworth drew attention in the Senate in more ways than one. In her first year, she introduced more bills than any other first-year senator. She also got her bills out of committee

Mothers may nurse their babies in public, but FAM required airports to give mothers the option of privacy.

more often than other first-year senators. To reach a vote in the Senate, a bill must first pass through a smaller group of senators, called a committee. Only then can the bill be voted on by the full Senate. Most bills stay in committee for a long time. But in her first two years, 10 of Duckworth's bills reached a Senate vote.

Duckworth drew more attention in 2018, when she became the first senator to give birth while in office. Taking care of a newborn while serving in the Senate was not easy. Duckworth planned to take 12 weeks off. But she also hoped to participate in important votes during her leave. However, senators were not allowed to bring babies onto the Senate floor. Women have faced many barriers to serving in Congress throughout history. As a result, the rules of Congress often did not accommodate the realities of many women's lives.

THINK ABOUT IT

As a woman, mother, and veteran, Duckworth brought a new perspective to Congress. How do you think this perspective benefited the Senate? How could it benefit the nation?

On April 19, 2018, Tammy Duckworth voted on the Senate floor with her baby, Maile.

To solve this problem, Duckworth pushed for a policy change. She succeeded. Less than two weeks after her daughter's birth, the Senate voted to allow babies onto the Senate floor. Senators would also be allowed to breastfeed their babies during votes. Thanks to Duckworth, the Senate took an important step in recognizing women as a permanent part of Congress.

POVERTY

Tammy Duckworth knows what it is like to face poverty. As a teenager, she watched her father struggle to find a job. She started working part-time to help her family. But the money from her jobs was not enough. To survive, her family depended on welfare. This is a type of financial support offered by the government.

Because of these struggles, Duckworth wanted to help low-income families. For example, Duckworth supported SNAP. This program is also known as food stamps. It provides funds to help low-income families buy food. Millions of families depend on SNAP to eat.

At times, the government has considered making changes to SNAP. One change would have excluded families that did not meet work requirements. Duckworth voted against this change. Another change would have prevented

In 2018, approximately 40 million people used SNAP across the United States.

immigrants who use SNAP from becoming US citizens. Duckworth also spoke out against this change. Duckworth did not think a person should have to go hungry to become a citizen.

Duckworth also worked for affordable childcare. In 2017, Duckworth helped introduce the Child Care for Working Families Act. This bill would give low-income families access to childcare. It did not pass the Senate. But in 2019, a group of senators reintroduced the bill.

ROHO.

CHAPTER 7

LOOKING AHEAD

Throughout her career, Tammy Duckworth set several records. She was the first female veteran with a disability to be elected to Congress. She was the second Asian American woman to become a senator. And she was the first woman to have a baby while serving in the Senate. As such, Duckworth has helped make politics more accessible to women, veterans, and people with disabilities.

In May 2019, Tammy Duckworth started leading a Senate task force to support female veterans.

In 2019, Duckworth had several bills in the works. In April, she put forward the Exercise and Fitness for All Act. This bill would create fitness opportunities for people with disabilities. In May, she introduced many other bills. These bills touched on the areas of education, public health, and energy.

Duckworth wanted to make progress in the Senate. But she also hoped to see change in the executive branch. As a senator, Duckworth often spoke out against President Donald Trump. She disagreed with his decisions on immigration and foreign affairs. For example, Duckworth believed Trump's actions toward Iran were dangerous.

Since 2018, Trump had taken actions that caused conflict with Iran. Some of Iran's responses increased that conflict. Duckworth thought Trump's actions risked leading the

Duckworth joins a protest against President Donald Trump's immigration policies.

United States into a war with Iran. In June 2019, she gave a speech opposing his actions.

As a senator, Duckworth spoke out against what she felt was wrong. She stood up for what she felt was right. She showed she was a great example of a groundbreaking woman in politics.

FOCUS ON

TAMMY DUCKWORTH

Write your answers on a separate piece of paper.

1. Write a paragraph describing how Tammy Duckworth's personal experiences could have affected her political goals.

2. Do you think Tammy Duckworth would make a good president? Why or why not?

3. In 2016, which politician did Tammy Duckworth defeat for her seat in the Senate?

  A. Dick Durbin
  B. Joe Walsh
  C. Mark Kirk

4. What type of jobs would law S. 496 likely create?

  A. governor jobs
  B. construction jobs
  C. military jobs

Answer key on page 48.

GLOSSARY

ambassador
An official representative of a country.

bill
A written plan to create or change a law.

combat
Fighting between armed forces.

conservative
Supporting traditional views or values, often resisting changes.

deployed
Called into military action.

food stamps
Also known as SNAP, funding from the government that low-income families can use to buy food.

incumbent
A politician currently serving in a certain position.

liberal
Supporting changes to traditional views or values to allow greater freedoms.

polls
Surveys that collect people's opinions on issues or elections.

prosthetic
Having to do with artificial body parts.

refugees
People forced to leave their homes due to war or other dangers.

TO LEARN MORE

BOOKS

Goldsmith, Connie. *Women in the Military: From Drill Sergeants to Fighter Pilots*. Minneapolis: Lerner Publishing Group, 2019.

Lanser, Amanda. *Women in Politics and Government*. Minneapolis: Abdo Publishing, 2017.

Sherman, Jill. *25 Women Who Fought Back*. North Mankato, MN: Capstone Press, 2019.

NOTE TO EDUCATORS

Visit **www.focusreaders.com** to find lesson plans, activities, links, and other resources related to this title.

INDEX

Answer Key: 1. Answers will vary; **2.** Answers will vary; **3.** C; **4.** B